Praise for Like One

"Like One... features plenty of great writing from poetry's big names, such as Emily Dickinson, Robert Frost, and William Carlos Williams, along with numerous modern writers as well, such as Dan Sklar, Doug Holder, Margaret Young, and Jill McDonough.... Pick up Like One: Poets for Boston; you'll be glad you did."
—Boston Poetry Magazine

"The City of Boston has shown great strength, unity and determination these past months as they recover from the devastation that occurred on April 15th. I was proud to learn that so many individuals with ties to New Jersey have shown support to Boston during this difficult time."
—Governor Chris Christie
on New Jersey poets' involvement in Like One

Like One: Poems For Boston

Like One

Poems For Boston

Edited by Deborah Finkelstein

Copyright © 2013 by Chocolate Chili Publishing
Published by Chocolate Chili Publishing, Boston, MA

All Rights Reserved

Cover designed using Wordle.net

Fonts used under SIL Open Font License Version 1.1:
  Cardo <http://www.fontsquirrel.com/fonts/Cardo>
  Chunkfive <http://www.fontsquirrel.com/fonts/ChunkFive>

Library of Congress Control Number: 2013944635

ISBN-13: 978-0989686907
ISBN-10: 0989686906

Dedicated to the memory of
Krystle Campbell,
Martin William Richard,
Lingzi Lu, and
Sean Collier,
and to all those who loved them

To all the victims of the Boston Marathon Bombing

To the first responders, medical professionals, and bystanders who assisted the injured

To everyone in need of healing

Acknowledgements

Several of the poems in this book were originally published, sometimes in different form, in the following journals, anthologies, or websites. Other poems were created for the following special celebrations. We are thankful to have them as part of the book.

"Accident, Mass Ave." by Jill McDonough. *Three Penny Review*, and *Where You Live* by Jill McDonough, Salt Publishing, 2012.

"Believing is Seeing" by Jan Seale. *A Quartet: Texas Poets in Concert* by R.S. Gwynn, Jan Seale, Naomi Shihab Nye, and William Virgil Davis, University of North Texas Press, 2000.

"The Body Corporeal" by Alfred Nicol. *Winter Light* by Alfred Nicol, University of Evansville Press, 2004.

"Cocktail Party" by Benjamin S. Grossberg. *Sweet Core Orchard* by Benjamin S. Grossberg, University of Tampa Press, 2009.

"Dust of Snow" by Robert Frost. *Yale Review*, 1921.

"Famous Kisses" by Joan Logghe. *The Singing Bowl* by Joan Logghe, University of New Mexico Press, 2011.

"Female Comic Book Superheroes" by Jeannine Hall Galley. *Becoming the Villainess* by Jeannine Hall Galley, Steel Toe Books, 2006.

"Immortal Longings" by Robert Pinsky. *The Want Bone* by Robert Pinsky, The Ecco Press, 1990.

"My Mother's Lipstick" by Lance Larson. *Cream City Review*.

"On Being a Nielsen Family" by Kevin Stein. *Sufficiency of the Actual* by Kevin Stein, University of Illinois Press, 2008.

"Primrose" by William Carlos Williams. *Poems* by William Carlos Williams, 1909.

"Roots and Wings" by Meghan Guidry was written as text for original music by Oliver Caplan <www.olivercaplan.com>, commissioned by the Handel Society of Dartmouth College <www.handelsociety.org>, Robert Duff, Artistic Director and Conductor, on the occasion of the Fiftieth Anniversary of the Hopkins Center for the Arts, 2012.

"The Rules of the New Car" by Wesley McNair. *Lovers of the Lost* by Wesley McNair, David R. Godine, 2010.

"A Sacrament" by Paulann Petersen. *A Bridge of Narrow Escape*, by Paulann Petersen, Cloudbank Books, 2006.

"Screen Porch" by Fred Marchant. *Full Moon Boat* by Fred Marchant, Graywolf Press, 2000.

"Secret Garden Trail" by Miriam Sagan. *Seven Places in America: A Poetic Sojourn* by Miriam Sagan, Sherman Asher Publishing, 2012.

"Sestri Levante" by Margaret Young. "30/30 Project," Tupelo Press.

"Simplicity" by Emily Dickinson. *The Poems of Emily Dickinson: Series Two.* 1896

"Some Thoughts on Rocks" by Jennifer Jean was originally written and recorded for the Winfisky Gallery's instillation "We're Standing On It: a Cross-Disciplinary Exhibition Inspired by Salem Gabbro" in March 2013.

"The Soul Fox" by David Mason. *The Virginia Quarterly Review.*

"Spring, This Ain't a Love Poem" by Doug Holder. *Seven Circles Press.*

"Summer, Shelling Peas" by Rusty Barnes. *The Dead Mule.*

"Sunday Evening" by David Trinidad. *Answer Song* by David Trinidad, High Risk Books/Serpent's Tail, 1994.

"Sunday Morning" by Nicolas Destino. *Heartwrecks* by Nicolas Destino, Sibling Rivalry Press, 2013.

"Under the Sun" by Cally Conan-Davies. *The Hudson Review.*

"What Were We Thinking?" by Maria Mazziotti Gillan. *North American Review*, and in her forthcoming book, T*he Silence in an Empty House*, NYQ Books, 2013.

"When I Heard the Learn'd Astronomer" by Walt Whitman. *Leaves of Grass* by Walt Whitman, 1900.

"A Woman Walks into a Bar" by Dan Sklar. *Flying Cats (Actually Swooping)* by Dan Sklar, Ibbetson Street Press, 2013.

I am honored to have so many wonderful poets as part of this book. I also wish to thank Brett Goldberg, publisher, for his tremendous help and support. I am grateful to my friends and colleagues for their advice and counsel, including Doug Holder, Sumita Mukerji, Will Fertman, Meghan Guidry, Donnelle McGee, Kat Good Schiff, Tracy Vicory-Rosenquist, Steve Glines, Linda Azrin, Alfonso Ramirez, Charles Hale, and Charles Rice-Gonzalez.

Contents

Introduction i

Poems

My Mother's Lipstick 1
   — Lance Larson

Famous Kisses 2
   — Joan Logghe

Female Comic Book Superheroes 3
   — Jeannine Hall Gailey

A Woman Walks Into A Bar 4
   — Dan Sklar

Cocktail Party 6
   — Benjamin S. Grossberg

Green Hills In Vermont 9
   — Donnelle McGee

Our Daily Walk, Amended 10
   — David Giver

Revere Beach After Hours 12
   — Kevin Carey

The Body Corporeal 14
   — Alfred Nicol

Sestri Levante 16
   — Margaret Young

Accident, Mass. Ave 17
   — Jill McDonough

In Summer My Father 19
   — Julie Kane

Screen Porch 20
   — Fred Marchant

Summer, Shelling Peas 21
   —Rusty Barnes

Under The Sun 22
   — Cally Conan-Davies

Simplicity 23
   — Emily Dickinson

Some Thoughts On Rocks 24
   — Jennifer Jean

Disco 26
   — Deborah Finkelstein

The Rules Of The New Car 27
   — Wesley McNair

On Being a Nielsen Family 28
   — Kevin Stein
Kudos 29
   — Judson Mitcham
Whoever You Are, Come Back 30
   — Caryn Mirriam-Goldberg
Roots and Wings 31
   — Meghan Guidry
The Soul Fox 32
   — David Mason
Believing Is Seeing 33
   — Jan Seale
When I Heard the Learn'd Astronomer 35
   —Walt Whitman
Immortal Longings 36
   — Robert Pinsky
Balance 37
   — Joy Ladin
Dust of Snow 38
   — Robert Frost
Yes 39
   — Debbi Brody
Primrose 40
   — William Carlos Williams
What Were We Thinking? 41
   — Maria Mazziotti Gillan
Lilacs 43
   — Kat Good-Schiff
A Sacrament 44
   — Paulann Petersen
Spring, This Ain't A Love Poem 45
   — Doug Holder
Secret Garden Trail 46
   — Miriam Sagan
Spirit of the Rain 47
   — Emily Pineau
Sunday Morning 49
   — Nicolas Destino
Sunday Evening 50
   — David Trinidad
Held 51
   — Aaron Jackson

Contributors 53

Introduction

Eight days after the Boston Marathon Bombing, I was at the Museum of Science when there was a sudden power outage. Flocks of elementary classes and other visitors were directed to the museum's lobby where there is plenty of natural light. Some of the students were quiet or were creating their own fun, such as one student who made sounds like an airplane and put out his arms to "take off." But other children were very serious, asking questions like, "Is it the bad guy?" "But I thought they got the bad guy." "Is he going to get us?" Eight days prior to that day the children would not have asked those questions, and had they, teachers would have immediately told them it was just a blackout. But these teachers were hesitant to reassure the students, hesitant to reassure themselves. Somewhere in their minds was a place where they too thought it was possible that it was the "bad guys."

The Boston Marathon Bombing has affected the way we see things. We have grown stronger, but we have also become more aware of the possibilities. We look differently at bags left unattended. We know it can happen here.

I wanted to help by creating an anthology of poems to raise money for The One Fund, the charity that helps the victims of the Boston Marathon Bombing and their families. People suggested that it should be a collection of poems about the events, but I disagreed. The community was not ready for such a book. There were still pictures being posted on Facebook, stories coming out from survivors being released from hospitals, signs hanging on utility poles memorializing the victims. Besides the community not being ready, most poets weren't either. Most poets, like most other folks, were still processing the event. Eventually there will be great poems about the event, and perhaps a collection of them. But today most are still healing.

This book is designed not just to raise money for The One Fund, which will literally be used to help people heal, it will also be used as a resource to help readers heal. I was inspired to choose poems that were positive and joyous, the way that other artists have used their craft to assist in healing a community while raising money for a cause such as the 12.12.12 concert that raised money for victims of Hurricane Sandy, or Comic Relief, a gathering of comedians and celebrities to raise money for the homeless or victims of Hurricane Katrina. Poetry is an incredible healing tool.

It's easy to see why some hospital and care facilities incorporate poetry projects. But it can also be used to heal all of us. Poetry creates catharsis. Its power is wrapped in the creative harnessing of raw emotion. It heals and nourishes the sprit while showing the mind a new way to view the world, and a new language to express that view. It allows people to connect in new ways, and generates new thought patterns, to heal.

I am blessed to have worked with so many talented people on this book. Poets were very receptive to the idea of a book that would be used to heal the community while raising money for The One Fund. As part of the healing process, poets were encouraged to send poems that healed and lifted the spirit with humor and joy. Some of the poems made me laugh out loud. Others took me on a journey through words and imagery that soothed my mind while stimulating my brain.

The poets in this book come from all over the country. They are a diverse blend of people with one common goal: building a better world. It was no surprise that the most common words used in the book were "like" and "one" because that describes us as a community. Poets came together like one.

Boston came together,

the country came together,

even the Yankees and the Red Sox came together

like one.

This is how we heal, by coming together and connecting. Poetry is part of that journey.

Like One

My Mother's Lipstick
— Lance Larson

They stood in raw rows of attention,
like retractable spies, a gallery of salmons
and pinks and racy reds
only an idiot would attempt to name.
She leaned into the mirror.
Someone had to witness this catechism
of the mouth, this transformation
from mother of four to femme fatale,
why not me? She'd go
at herself, like someone reviving
a damaged masterpiece, all dab and blot,
then lip down softly on a piece
of tissue. For a moment, that red dream
floated in two places at once,
on her pursed mouth and on a pane
of white—a perfectly good movie star
kiss flushed away, goodbye,
making promises to beauty no shade
on earth could ever duplicate.
My sister playing Solitaire, my father
buried in the sky on some business trip.
I alone in that workshop of mirrors,
that boudoir of wet sighs, taking in
before and after—the mystery
of a lustrous she who spoke my name,
whose mouth was plum
perfect, waiting and refusing to be kissed.

FAMOUS KISSES
   — Joan Logghe

"fare well perfect mammal.
Fare thee well, from thy silken couch and dark day!"
   – Michael McClure, Ghost Tantras 39

if I had to choose between kissing Marilyn Monroe
or Einstein I would be stumped. I'd pick Marilyn of course
for her lips had the attention of America, had that much charge
and Joe DiMaggio's home run in them, Arthur Miller's last
line, and they kissed Clark Gable and felt his moustache.
I know that Marilyn tasted of purple conversation hearts,
those packets of candy with slang you buy for Valentine's
and the purple, like her lipstick, a little bitter.
Einstein is meanwhile tapping me on the shoulder, whispering
"Space is love" in my left ear. But Marilyn has me now
with her one shoe dangling from her toe and the eternal
subway grate blowing up under her dress and her legs also
part of the way she kisses. I'm melting at Marilyn's moist
overture, her apertures like Nikon cameras in dim light,
wide open. Kissing Marilyn is American as a California
morning. It's reels of film in silver cans that only live
for screens. Light breaks out. Peace breaks out. Death
breaks me open and I'm kissing Marilyn Monroe to learn to be
the best kisser in America. Then Einstein gets my attention.
He tickles me with his white erotic hair, hair
with the energy of atom, of microwave. I can feel
him through my clothes. And for one minute I turn from
the perfect mammal to the man of mind over matter. I lean
over to him. He kisses me on the cheek. I become younger.
I love backwards. My heart is a ten year old's and I'm traveling
through space into a perfect equation of love.

FEMALE COMIC BOOK SUPERHEROES
— Jeannine Hall Gailey

are always fighting evil in a thong,
pulsing techno soundtrack in the background
as their tiny ankles thwack

against the bulk of male thugs.
With names like Buffy, Elektra, or Storm
they excel in code decryption, Egyptology, and pyrotechnics.

They pout when tortured, but always escape just in time,
still impeccable in lip gloss and pointy-toed boots,
to rescue male partners, love interests, or fathers.

Impossible chests burst out of tight leather jackets,
from which they extract the hidden scroll or antidote,
tousled hair covering one eye.

They return to their day jobs as forensic pathologists,
wearing their hair up, donning dainty glasses.
Of all the goddesses, these pneumatic heroines most

resemble Artemis, with her miniskirts and crossbow,
or Freya, with her giant gray cats.
Each has seen this apocalypse before.

See her perfect three-point landing on top of the chariot,
riding the silver moon into the horizon,
city crumbling around her heels.

A WOMAN WALKS INTO A BAR
— Dan Sklar

The woman walks
down the street quickly,
heels clacking on the sidewalk
nervous confidence the dignity
of having a place to go
and comes to the place
and pulls open the door
with long swift motions,
leaning back other arm
reaching way out swinging
a counter balance, walks in,
does not look around,
sits at the bar.
She orders a drink
even though the bartender
knows what it is.
These are the moments
she loves: the walk to the bar,
the door, the bartender
knowing what she drinks,
waiting for the drink
in the warm dark place
and dark wooden bar
with the little lights and
glasses and bottles sparkling
and the clinking of the glasses
and bottles and ice cubes.
The first sip is the best
and they are all good.
When the drink comes
she doesn't drink it right away.
When the night is through
her back is straighter than before
sort of half almost smile,
eyes in a new place.
She pushes open the door

and the air hits her face.
She goes left and walks
half a block. Stops, smiles
to herself with some
of her mouth—turns around
and goes the other way.

COCKTAIL PARTY
— Benjamin S. Grossberg

I wouldn't be afraid of dying if there were a mere
four-hour event—drinks, let's say, hors d'oeuvres—
at the end of the world. I would arrive early, if possible,
wearing shoes that peg me for the early 1990s
and the nice things I hope they bury me in.
I'd get my drink—vodka soda, lime—grab
a full plate of grapes from the fruit trays, fresh
off those vines still growing
at the end of the world, then begin my rounds.

The first thing of course will be to hear all the news,
to give some and to hear some. The last days
of Pompeii, yes. Maybe I'll tell someone
how the people left cool impressions on the walls.
The Roman Empire? Finite.
I could talk a little about Germanic hordes,
then point a few noble Romans toward better sources.
Someone could tell me how the ice caps fared,
how the American experiment finally turned out,
if the gray wolves made it, if anyone ever read
anything I wrote, what happened
to my brother's children, and to my last dog. But

who knows if I'll be able to find anyone
with my personal news. It will be a big room.
I may have to settle for the cosmic: did the Democrats
ever retake Congress? How did we manage
once fossil fuels ran out? I will not look
for Shakespeare, no doubt at the center
of a large crowd on one of the balconies; I will not

hang out with Kenneth Starr, alone at one of the bars,
even when I go back to refill my glass. I will also

not be polite if I see anyone I knew but didn't like.
This is the end of the world we're talking about.
I'll have risen from a very long wait in the grave
and no doubt will not be in the mood to have any more
of my time wasted. If I meet a Viking,
I may ask about the journey across the Atlantic
in a long boat. If I happen on my mother
I'll probably pose my few lingering questions
about the cruelties she inflicted on me in childhood.
But that's it. Mostly I just want to know
that we all made it out together—
if not alive—and that we all can mingle
in one large room, listening to a single four-piece,
sipping really big drinks mixed by the angels.

I guess I just want the assurance right now,
before time goes even one bit further,
that I'll get to come back at the very end—
that I'll be filled in about all the things I missed,
and that if, between this time and that one,
there is anyone who I learn to love,
I'll be able to find him there, too.

No doubt he'll be looking for me, expecting me
by the fruit trays. When the lights dim
and the barkeeps announce last call,
angels will walk around with shawls

and formal coats draped over one celestial arm,
Inuit furs, togas and muu-muus over the other,

and thank each guest for coming, as we trudge back out
to our coffins, to buckle up snug before
the colossally violent contraction
that will be the end of the world.

I will take my friend's hand, and make one last pass
at the hors d'oeuvres table. If he's a gentleman,
he'll open my coffin first and wait for me to get in
before walking around to his own.
I'd be happy then, I think, settling in, knowing
that everything finally turned out all right.

GREEN HILLS IN VERMONT
— Donnelle McGee

This is how I can save myself
    Like this —

Listening to Cocker belt *With A Little Help From My Friends*,

Reading Neruda.

Kissing the red and black medicine bag I keep tucked in my pant pocket.

Eating strawberries off her flat, white, pierced belly.

Visiting upstate New York, summer after summer . . . after summer.

Running up and down them green hills in Vermont,
For here is where my third eye resides.

Looking at hummingbirds . . . my kids making pancakes.

OUR DAILY WALK, AMENDED
— David Giver

The path was routine, full of routines,
Of my daughter and I, hand in hand,
Playing never ending games of "I spy".

She the master and I the novice,
My play never good enough to not fall
Victim to a retelling of the constantly in flux rules.

Then we pause, sprint across the empty street,
And make our way to the circus,
A circus where she is the headlining acrobat

Confidently walking the retaining wall tight rope
With all of the grace in the world,
Steadied by my hand,

That is grasped onto when balance is lost,
But that is swatted at most other times
As she knows what she is doing.

Her dismount leaves us just steps away
From the local market, the market that sells the only cookies
That could possibly fuel her way home,

And she coyly demands a stop at the market, later.
She spots her friend, Sandy, who we cordially greet
With curtseys and bows

She takes from the sand that makes up the bed
For the massive concrete form of Sandy
And uses it to feed the colossus. A quick hug

And we are on our way, as the true reason,
The whole point of our walk,
Is about to be realized.

We reach our rocky perch, the one from which we watch the surfers
Navigate the edge of the continent, just in time
To see the sun rise up over the waters of the bay

An action that we assume has happened
Each and every day, but this is the first either of us
Can remember being present at that moment
when night becomes day.

REVERE BEACH AFTER HOURS
— Kevin Carey

It's after midnight, still 90 degrees,
the customers are twenty deep
at each window, most of them drunk,
all of them on the make
all of them hungry.
We push food at them like one might
throw meat at a wild bear:
fried clams, roast beef sandwiches,
lobster rolls.
The more they eat, the more they
come, the line feeding on itself and growing,
like the Blob in the Steve McQueen movie,
or some Trojan war flick
where the soldiers keep coming
in waves no matter how many
arrows they take.
The crowd swells after the bars
break and the people
are more drunk with each order,
and a girl and a guy make out
in the front of the line
and someone yells get a room
and a white Cadillac pulls up
to the curb and turns a radio loud.
They all start dancing, long hair,
tight pants, hips moving to the disco beat,
Boogie Oogie Oogie, and a plane
flies low overhead on its way
to East Boston and the sway gets
louder with the laughter and the sidewalk
moves with the motion
and the madness, and for a moment I stop
what I am doing and stand with
my hands on my hips, the food
hot and waiting behind me.

I stare at the bobbing heads,
the hungry mouths,
the wave of temporary joy
against the dark ocean across the street.

THE BODY CORPOREAL
— Alfred Nicol

The owner comes to greet
This customer, who'll eat
More at a sitting than
Entire families can.
I watched him as he ate
A pizza, then a plate
Of pasta, chicken wings
And several other things
So quickly that I knew
He wasn't nearly through
His appetizer yet!
The waitress went to get
Another tray of stuff,
And I had had enough
 Just watching him, and so
I stood up then to go
And wondered, as I stood,
Just how on earth he could
Get up out of his seat
When all he'd had to eat
Had settled down to where
He's closest to the chair
(Though where that chair might be
Was difficult to see).
Anyway, I went home.

I didn't write this poem
Or think to write it then,
But only later when
The DPW
Began jackhammering through
The street outside my door,
And as it shook my floor
I ventured out to see
What all the noise could be.
Then I laid eyes on what

God meant with such a butt
On such a man. His load
Of flesh upon the road
Was an apparent good,
Abundant where it stood
The one unshaken thing
Amid the thundering,
At peace there, hunched around
That hurricane of sound
That made the branches fall
But fazed him not at all.
The tool looked like a toy
Held by an older boy
Than it was meant to please.
Like mighty limbs of trees
Beneath their trembling leaves,
His arms within his sleeves
Ignored the flapping shirt,
The flying rocks and dirt.
Without fatigue or wrath
He held a steady path,
As certain as the sun,
And worked till he was done
With cutting up the street.
He went somewhere to eat.

Sestri Levante
— Margaret Young

Across the peninsula from where Byron
swam (according to the plaque)

in a park one hotel away from the beach
(seashell fountains, two small playgrounds)

flanked by rows of coin-op rides (Apache helicopter,
dragon, mule with hillbilly hat and jug of hooch)

there is this little carousel: monster truck,
princess coach, Formula One race car

all glitter and chrome, swarming with
airbrushed unlicensed characters.

The operator takes our euro, smokes,
and plays Snoop Dogg each time

we go there, "Gin and Juice" once
and another time a newer one,

something about bitches as my son
and Italian kids ride circles, waving.

The sea is Dora Markus here, and Shelley.
We all watch it snuff out one night's sun.

My son says he'll remember. What,
I ask. Everything, he says.

ACCIDENT, MASS. AVE.
— Jill McDonough

I stopped at a red light on Mass. Ave.
in Boston, a couple blocks away
from the bridge, and a woman in a beat-up
old Buick backed into me. Like, cranked her wheel,
rammed right into my side. I drove a Chevy
pickup truck. It being Boston, I got out
of the car yelling, swearing at this woman,
a little woman, whose first language was not English.
But she lived and drove in Boston, too, so she knew,
we both knew, that the thing to do
is get out of the car, slam the door
as hard as you fucking can and yell things like *What the fuck
were you thinking? You fucking blind? What the fuck
is going on? Jesus Christ!* So we swore
at each other with perfect posture, unnaturally angled
chins. I threw my arms around, sudden
jerking motions with my whole arms, the backs
of my hands toward where she had hit my truck.
But she hadn't hit my truck. She hit
the tire; no damage done. Her car
was fine, too. We saw this while
we were yelling, and then we were stuck.
The next line in our little drama should have been
*Look at this fucking dent! I'm not paying for this
shit. I'm calling the cops, lady.* Maybe we'd throw in a
You're in big trouble, sister, or *I just hope for your sake
there's nothing wrong with my fucking suspension,* that
sort of thing. But there was no fucking dent. There
was nothing else for us to do. So I
stopped yelling, and she looked at the tire she'd
backed into, her little eyebrows pursed
and worried. She was clearly in the wrong, I was enormous,
and I'd been acting as if I'd like to hit her. So I said

*Well, there's nothing wrong with my car, nothing wrong
with your car...are you OK?* She nodded, and started
to cry, so I put my arms around her and I held her, middle
of the street, Mass. Ave., Boston, a couple blocks from the bridge.
I hugged her, and I said *We were scared, weren't we?*
and she nodded and we laughed.

In Summer My Father
— Julie Kane

In summer my father came to life
Like the seeds of purple clover under the lawn
Like the seeds of Queen Anne's lace under roadside meadows

In summer my father stood knee-deep
In the sea that could not drown him, being born in a sailor's caul
In the bracing Atlantic, and cupped his hands and drank

In summer my father's copper freckles
Merged into a tan, though my own would never do it
Merged, and the golden fuzz stood up on the backs of his fingers

In summer my father grew tomatoes
Setting aside his papers to scratch in the backyard soil
Setting aside his cocktail and Viceroy cigarettes

In summer my father followed baseball
Hearing the Boston Red Sox on a crackling transistor radio
Hearing the echoes of cheers for his hits at Melrose High School

In summer my father joined his buddies
Sunday mornings plucking a golf shirt from the rainbow in his closet
Sunday evenings slinking home beery, his pockets full of stubby pencils

In summer my father banished winter
Banished tunneling into snowbanks to sleep in France and Belgium
Banished lighting a fire in his helmet, in the sleet, in Nazi Germany

In summer my mother took to her room with a book
Complaining that she felt faint, that it might be a touch of heatstroke
Complaining of poison ivy, of an ear infected from swimming

But in summer my father came to life

SCREEN PORCH
    — Fred Marchant

Summer nights I loved the cool pillow
 as it settled into dampness,

the city noise as it dwindled,
the smell of plants, lights in the apartment

across the street going out. Crickets.
First light had to be inferred from shadows

slipping off locusts, and tall wild sumacs,
from wet sparkles in the mesh,

a daddy longlegs looking right at you.

Summer, Shelling Peas
   —Rusty Barnes

There are old ladies all along
this stretch of road shelling peas
into plastic buckets in the late
five 'o'clock heat and you sit on
this porch in a lawn chair with one
your cutoff jeans and halter top
out of place horribly
in the chaff-dust day
the peas like tiny hearts
in your hand. You roll them out
of the pod with your thumb
and they tinkle like rain
into the bucket. We drink
iced tea and eat chips
as the last strains of daylight
fall. We play euchre under
the bug-zapper at the picnic table
and later that night I take
your thumb into my mouth
and taste you,
and the good earth.

UNDER THE SUN
— Cally Conan-Davies

Taking an hour from time-and-again

I offer the sun the gold of my skin.

Brushed by a breeze of couldn't-care-less

I rest my head on my rolled-up dress,

till all of give is shift at my hips

and all of need is salt on my lips

and all of time is the tidal span

and all I am,

an impression in sand.

SIMPLICITY
— Emily Dickinson

How happy is the little stone
That rambles in the road alone,
And doesn't care about careers
And exigencies never fears—
Whose coat of elemental brown
A passing universe put on,
And independent as the sun
Associates or glows alone,
Fulfilling absolute decree
In casual simplicity—

SOME THOUGHTS ON ROCKS.
— Jennifer Jean

Which came first, the rock or the poem?

Ruth Stone (real name) says the poem
is
floating above us
coalescing like the unborn,
like ball lightning,
and if we don't run from the field to the desk
it won't inhabit us, erupt
from our pen.
It will spin away, bolt, to another
more willing more ready more swift
poet, or as some would say—
parent.

Ruth Stone wasn't much for research.
Whereas, I
know
I wanted to write about rocks,
so I look up how to make and wake
a model volcano
because
the only thing interesting about rock is how to
destroy it—
and those in the know
say you've got to heat it like a Mother
Earth's mantle chamber
to soften rock into magma.
Which I can't do, really, hence
the model—hence, *the remove*.

Y'know,
my son would like even fake magma.
He wouldn't care if it's just
water soap coloring vinegar
in a drink bottle—then, baking soda in a tissue
dropped into that bottle. "We *killed* it!"
I see us crowing.
And because I imagine the completed feat,
I feel a kind of triumph,
an easy triumph. Is that Ruth Stone's floating poem?
Is it like looking with love at
a gripped, mute photo
of your grinning kid—versus looking in
their eyes for real?

If that's Ruthy's schtick, that's sad.
Can't we both be right? Like how I got a C-section—
because I think too much.
It took two days of Mount Vesuvian pain, a spinal tap, and a slice,
to get this—rather cute—baby out.
While (true story here)
my more fluid friends
pulled into the nearest hospital parking lot,
where she *hhheeeee-
hhheeeeed* and *hwooooo-
hwooooooood*
through some "pressure" for ten minutes in the backseat
as he drove with his knees—
his left hand on the cell to the nurse,
his right hand reaching back
in time to catch
the baby.

DISCO
— Deborah Finkelstein

When I was born
everyone was disco dancing,
bright colored lights
mapping pathways to eyes,
pointing fingers to the moon,
arching bodies like warriors,
spinning like they could
change the rotation of the planet.
They say this era ended
or never existed,
a purge of clothing
dumped in a truck,
college kids sneak it
out for 70's parties,
wondering why the collars
are so wide,
necklines so deep,
medallions so heavy.
I stare at the 70's photos,
the odd woman in polyester
bell bottoms, oversized glasses,
the strange man in the leisure suit,
mullet and giant mustache,
wondering why my baby album
has no pictures
of my parents.

The Rules Of The New Car
— Wesley McNair

After I got married and became
the stepfather of two children, just before
we had two more, I bought it, the bright
blue sorrowful car that slowly turned
to scratches and the flat black spots
of gum in the seats and stains impossible
to remove from the floor mats. Never again,
I said as our kids, four of them by now,
climbed into the new car. This time,
there will be rules. The first to go
was the rule I made for myself about
cleaning it once a week, though why,
I shouted at the kids in the rearview mirror,
should I have to clean it if they would just
remember to fold their hands. Three years
later, it was the same car I had before,
except for the dent my wife put in the grille
when, ignoring the regulation about snacks,
she reached for a bag of chips on her way
home from work and hit a tow truck. Oh,
the ache I felt for the broken rules,
and the beautiful car that had been lost,
and the car that we now had, on soft
shocks in the driveway, still unpaid for.
Then one day, for no particular reason except
that the car was loaded down with wood
for the fireplace at my in-laws' camp
and groceries and sheets and clothes
for the week, my wife in the passenger seat,
the dog lightly panting beside the kids in the back,
all innocent anticipation, waiting for me
to join them, I opened the door to my life.

ON BEING A NIELSEN FAMILY
— Kevin Stein

We pocket five ones when we agree,
fingered cash our soul's ransom.
And a Family Viewership Record Book
for each TV, of which we've three.
We are the Postmodern Descartes,

pledging, "I watch, therefore I am."
We're the grand experiment that was
America, both scientist and the mouse
with a human ear stitched to its pink back,
checking the appropriate idiot-box boxes.

We're our own Peeping Tom, peering in.
On stage, we're culture's disguise,
the way a bickering couple makes nice
once the bell ding-dongs neighbors in
for cocktails and unsalted Cheese Nips.

Though it's Oprah, we circle BBC News.
Though Jerry Springer, we mark Charlie Rose.
No no no. Not South Park, not Cops,
not World's Funniest Animal Tricks,
but History Channel and Discovery,

NASA Live, Nightline, and Devotionals,
the Food Network's Thanksgiving Day
Vegan Special. We are watched watching,
watching ourselves watched. We are never
enough, so the lie is as we wish to be.

KUDOS
— Judson Mitcham

But why no praise for the lazy,
no kudos for the slow, no hallelujahs
for those of us who do so little, no trophy

for performance on the sofa,
for snack-related achievement,
for freestyle in the long nap category,
for world-class work with the remote?

Why no certificate for energy savings
at the level of the calorie, no laurel
for best excuse? Who appreciates

how much effort there is in sloth,
how much sad truth there is in inertia,
how hard the heart does start to work?
Surely, there's a prize for us, a sideways

accolade made of lead
for those of us who are always tired
and going back to bed.

WHOEVER YOU ARE, COME BACK
— Caryn Mirriam-Goldberg

This is what the waters always tell us: rolling away from
and toward us in the dark, reminding us of everything
that formed us in the darkness before our cells even
clustered enough toward some kind of knowing.
The shine in the sky, on the lake speaks light to
light to what climbs in the core of our spines.
Not so much in words, but in a language composed
of rain, longing, glimmer above, depth below,
and horizons beyond too far to comprehend.

This storm lands, face to face, in the center of this pond:
this dream we return to, recognizing the lapis moment
that the stars burn through the thinning skin of the clouds.
Whoever is lost is found here. Whatever lines old loves
followed or lost sight of no longer bind us apart.
Let us hear this wind, feel it sweep our faces clean
in the beating heart of the world. Let us return.

ROOTS AND WINGS
— Meghan Guidry

We marked our paths in autumn's fallen flame
where feet scattered birds from branch, a span
of feathers in flight, their source is the same:
A beginning, shared, for every coming plan.

Our arches learned to trod cool brick and pine.
The ground of fire leaves an afterglow
of golden green and clockwork stir, a time
beneath the skin and winter's silver snow.

The cold cannot erase the home akin
to lines of lives like roots in distant ground.
And though dispersed, we hold our kindred skin
like wings to carry us in common sound.

Our calls spread the arms of this single star,
weaves where we were to where we always are.

THE SOUL FOX
— David Mason

for Chrissy, 28 October 2011

My love, the fox is in the yard.
The snow will bear his print a while,
then melt and go, but we who saw
his way of finding out, his night
of seeking, know what we have seen
and are the better for it. Write.
Let the white page bear the mark,
then melt with joy upon the dark.

BELIEVING IS SEEING
— Jan Seale

And these signs shall follow them that believe...
Mark 16:17

Eyes that have tracked rabbits, birds, deer
all afternoon across the simple oak
now tear and smart, ready as they are
to discover in the cold Hill Country night
Orion among the hot uncompromising stars.
The astronomer emerges from his lens.
"We have a treat tonight," my son says
and waits until a plane has closed its path.
"First you find Orion by his belt."
His finger points me to the spangled girth.
And then we telescope the Great Hunter:
the yellow-red on his right shoulder named
Betelgeuse, a pulsing variable giant,
and Bellatrix on his left; straight down
find Rigel, making his knee a blue-white glint.
We shiver and our breaths form nebulae
of no order. "The next stars"--my son smiles--
"we'll see together. I have to show you how."
I <u>will</u> to see beyond the late night books,
the fog of years, the dimming earthly weather.
"Beside the sword you'll see a cloudy mass."
I strain through waves and jerks from here to there,
search Orion's skirt for starry soil.
The cloud mass finally settles to its place.
"You mean the thing that looks like printers' dots?"
"Orion's Nebula," the astronomer says,
then stands against me firm to make a brace.
"Keep looking, Mom. For now, just blink and stare.
I promise you will see them if you try,
wow..wow.and hope--yes, hope for three bright stars."
Minutes go by. The click of the telescope timer
corrects what we cannot--our restless ride
on this galloping star-drenched porch.

And then the gift: three clear and perfect points,
three diamond apples where none were before.
Afraid to blink, I whisper, "Yes, I see them.
Yes." The astronomer's hand tightens on my arm.
"The Trapezium Cluster, at fifteen-hundred light-years."
He laughs. "I give them to you because you see them."
"I take them," I say, and feel him near.

WHEN I HEARD THE LEARN'D ASTRONOMER
—Walt Whitman

When I heard the learn'd astronomer,
When the proofs, the figures, were ranged in columns before me,
When I was shown the charts and diagrams, to add, divide, and measure them,
When I sitting heard the astronomer where he lectured with much applause in the lecture-room,
How soon unaccountable I became tired and sick,
Till rising and gliding out I wander'd off by myself,
In the mystical moist night-air, and from time to time,
Look'd up in perfect silence at the stars.

IMMORTAL LONGINGS
— Robert Pinsky

Inside the silver body
Slowing as it banks through veils of cloud
We float separately in our seats

Like the cells or atoms of one
Creature, needs
And states of a shuddering god.

Under him, a thirsty brilliance.
Pulsing or steady,
The fixed lights of the city

And the flood of carlights coursing
Through the grid: Delivery,
Arrival, Departure. Whim. Entering

And entered. Touching
And touched: down
The lit boulevards, over the bridges

And the river like an arm of night.
Book, cigarette. Bathroom.
Thirst. Some of us are asleep.

We tilt roaring
Over the glittering
Zodiac of intentions.

BALANCE
   — Joy Ladin

It's always evening somewhere, and now the evening is mine.
Summer's over, I'm moving on,
the shuddering pans of the scale subside.
I didn't fail, I was right on time,
the perfect balance is undisturbed
by the angst still elbowing on either side.
I'm done with weighing and being weighed. Goodbye!
I soar like a balloon a child let fly.
The little void I held inside
opens into sky.

DUST OF SNOW
— Robert Frost

The way a crow
Shook down on me
The dust of snow
From a hemlock tree

Has given my heart
A change of mood
And saved some part
Of a day I had rued.

YES
   — Debbi Brody

Today, a no-bad-news day,
a field of yellow asters
interspersed with late purples,
a sky calling out the fizz
and fling of Autumn's equinox.

Dirt in my sandals, a jiggle
of earth salad. In the rapture
of unbuttoned daylight, a dance
with a witless audience,
an eruption of yes.

PRIMROSE
  — William Carlos Williams

Yellow, yellow, yellow, yellow!
It is not a color.
It is summer!
It is the wind on a willow,
the lap of waves, the shadow
under a bush, a bird, a bluebird,
three herons, a dead hawk
rotting on a pole--
Clear yellow!
It is a piece of blue paper
in the grass or a threecluster of
green walnuts swaying, children
playing croquet or one boy
fishing, a man
swinging his pink fists
as he walks--
It is ladysthumb, forget-me-nots
in the ditch, moss under
the flange of the carrail, the
wavy lines in split rock, a
great oaktree--
It is a disinclination to be
five red petals or a rose, it is
a cluster of birdsbreast flowers
on a red stem six feet high,
four open yellow petals
above sepals curled
backward into reverse spikes--
Tufts of purple grass spot the
green meadow and clouds the sky.

WHAT WERE WE THINKING?
— Maria Mazziotti Gillan

In 1972, I loved orange, a color I thought suited me
as blue did my blonde sister-in-law. So when we replaced
the dirty pinky-gray carpet that came with our house,
I bought a deep orange shag, the living room and dining
room both large rooms, covered in acres of bright orange.

To add to the effect, I painted the walls harvest moon,
a lighter shade than the carpet but still orange
after all, and lastly, I bought a deep orange chair
and an orange cheese platter with a sunflower painted
in the middle where I plopped a slab of orange cheddar

and surrounded it with crackers and served it to the other
couples who visited us on Saturday evenings—Judy and Al,
Mary Ellen and Vic, Laura and Fred, Bob and Bette.
For the final touch, I added an orange fondue pot
with a flame cup underneath. Inside, melted orange cheddar

cheese I served with French bread. Perfect! In our bright
orange universe, I thought I had arrived, moved away
from the drab tenement where I grew up, the colorless
world of my mother's house. I dressed in a long skirt
and silk blouse, or bell-bottom lounging pants

and blouses with balloon sleeves secured by tight cuffs.
You wore a shirt with flowers on it, a tapered shirt
that showed off your wide shoulders and narrow waist.
The children peeked at us from the curve in the stairs.
We had gin and tonics and scotch and sodas and we'd talk
and laugh and I thought I was sophisticated, rising
toward the upper class. The brightness of those rooms
felt as if I had taken the sun and brought it inside, which,
because of the big oaks that surrounded our house,
was always dark. Imagine us there together, both of us
thirty-two years old, our children finally asleep in their beds,
surrounded by our friends.

We had so much of our lives ahead of us, and the future,
we are certain, is as bright and full of possibilities
as the room. Nothing can stop us. We cannot imagine
a time when we will look back
at ourselves and laugh at how much
we had yet to learn, how little we knew.

LILACS
  — Kat Good-Schiff

let's plant them
near our bedroom
she said
so we'll smell them
in the spring
when we first open
the windows

I said yes
and even though
we had no house of our own
no soil
not even a window
we smelled them
every spring day

A SACRAMENT
— Paulann Petersen

Become that high priest,
the bee. Drone your way
from one fragrant
temple to another, nosing
into each altar. Drink
what's divine—
and while you're there,
let some of the sacred
cling to your limbs.
Wherever you go
leave a small trail
of its golden crumbs.

In your wake
the world unfolds
its rapture, the fruit
of its blooming.
Rooms in your house
fill with that sweetness
your body both
makes and eats.

SPRING, THIS AIN'T A LOVE POEM
— Doug Holder

Oh for crying out loud
It is here again.
The tulips sprout
Like maddening clichés...
Those
Blooming idiots!
And the chirp
Of those morning birds,
What are we left with
Their pellets, their
Turds.

And some chick
In the Square
Says she smells the fragrance
Of love in the air.

A professor
In Harvard Yard
Tells his students
"Hope springs eternal'
Well, pal
I won't put that
In my journal.

Damn you spring!
You swept away
The cold insular
Comforts of my winter's day.

SECRET GARDEN TRAIL
— Miriam Sagan

Why must inspiration be a vista?
Remembered peonies are beaten down by rain
Into their impressionistic essence.
A formal garden in the mind's eye
Blurs in all this mist
And the dark alley between trees
Is scattered with pine cones, cinquefoil, trillium.
In a sculpture garden
Even the mushrooms
Seem placed on purpose.
Once, half-lost, I turned in a cul de sac
And saw through a gap
A pond full of water lilies
In all directions--
An inner self
That also shifts shape.

SPIRIT OF THE RAIN
— Emily Pineau

There is something
very calming about rain
even when
it gets really thick
and out of control.

The line between the road
and the pond is blurred.
But Brian pulls to a gentle
stop, as the windshield wipers
do the best they can do.

A bird with a long neck
is standing at the edge
of the water.
It reminds me of a swan,
but its body isn't full enough.

Darkness, blurred vision.
The bird seems to be
grey or white.
"I think that's a crane,"
Brian says.
"Or maybe a heron".
We stare into the path
of the headlights
as though we've never
seen a bird before.

Native Americans believe
that a grey heron
brings good luck.
Especially if you see one
take flight.

The moment the windshield wipers
clear the view,
Brian snaps a picture.
The soaked bird
spreads its wings
and takes off into the rain.

Sunday Morning
— Nicolas Destino

When you live alone you can put things where you wish.
Alone, you can contaminate your own environment and spill
olive oil on an orange floating in the sink. You can
sink where you want to, in your own particles, part the
water, create miracles. You can say *excuse the mess...would you like
a drink?* When you live alone you are naked more often. If another
man is naked with you in bed, you can say *welcome visitor*. If
another man contaminates your environment, you can say *thanks
for coming over*, and you can clean up after him with old rags only
you know where to find.

SUNDAY EVENING
— David Trinidad

Back from Boston,
Ira and I listen
to a tape of Anne Sexton
reading her poems—
part of my $87.00 binge
at the Grolier Book Shop
in Harvard Square.
Ira likes her "smoky" voice,
which is interrupted
by the kettle's shrill whistle.
I go into the kitchen
and prepare our tea:
Cranberry Cove for Ira,
Mellow Mint for me.
We sip, smoke and listen
to Anne. Toward the end
of the tape, Ira unpacks
the little black bag
of Godiva chocolates
and, one by one, eats
a butterscotch-filled coat
of arms, a light brown starfish
and a gold-foiled cherry cordial.
He chews and smiles.
I regret that I ate all
of mine on the train.
But wait! He offers me
his last one (which he
makes me earn with kisses):
a dark chocolate heart.

HELD
— Aaron Jackson

Bent into the fold
My body lies in hers
Wrapped into a ball
Bound by the pledge of the ring
We lay in unity
Forgetting the turbulence of the world

Outside the window
Chaos attempts to invade

Her feet are cold
My calves are warm
She likes the feeling of warmth

When woman holds man the moment is remembered
As though the timelessness of vulnerability
Cannot be forgotten

Contributors

Rusty Barnes lives and writes in Revere MA. He is about to publish his third and fourth books, and is working on a chapbook of poems about his adopted city, Revere MA.

Debbi Brody conducts poetry workshops and readings at festivals and other venues throughout the Southwest, for writers and listeners age five to ninety-five. She publishes in regional and national literary journals as well as numerous anthologies of note. Her new chapbook, Awe in the Muddle, is available via email at <artqueen58@aol.com>, subject: chapbook.

Kevin Carey teaches in the English Department at Salem State University and is a part-time filmmaker. His new book of poetry is *The One Fifteen to Penn Station*. His latest documentary film, about New Jersey poet Maria Mazziotti Gillan, is called *All That Lies Between Us*.

Cally Conan-Davies is an Australian poet now living in Colorado and Oregon. Her work has appeared in *Poetry, The Hudson Review, The New Criterion, The Sewanee Review, The Southwest Review* and many other magazines. She is married to poet David Mason.

Nicolas Destino, originally from Niagara Falls, New York, is a poet and essayist whose work includes a co-authored chapbook, *Of Kingdoms & Kangaroo*, and essay, "Travel of Sound," which received notable mention in the Best American Essays series. Destino currently lives in Montclair, New Jersey. <www.nicolasdestino.com>

Born in Amherst, **Emily Dickinson** attended Amherst Academy and then studied at Mount Holyoke Female Seminary. Less than a dozen of **Emily Dickinson**'s poems were published during her lifetime, but after her death, hundreds of poems were found and published. Books include *Bolts of Melody, Final Harvest,* and *The Single Hound*.

Deborah Finkelstein teaches creative writing at North Shore Community College and Endicott College. Recent publications include *Lummox, Ibbetson Street, Magnolia,* and *Cradle Songs.* She also writes haiku and plays. <www.DeborahFinkelstein.com>

Robert Frost received four Pulitzer Prizes for Poetry, and the U.S. Congressional Gold Medal. His poetry collections include *North of Boston, New Hampshire, A Witness Tree, A Further Range, Steeple Bush, A Boy's Will,* and *In the Clearing.* He spent many years living, writing, and teaching in New England.

Jeannine Hall Gailey is the Poet Laureate of Redmond, Washington and the author of three books, *Becoming the Villainess, She Returns to the Floating World,* and her latest, *Unexplained Fevers.* Her web site is <www.webbish6.com>

Maria Mazziotti Gillan won the 2011 Barnes & Noble Writers for Writers Award and the 2008 American Book Award. She is Founder /Executive Director of the Poetry Center at Passaic County Community College, editor of *Paterson Literary Review,* and Director of the Creative Writing Program/Professor of Poetry at Binghamton University-SUNY. She has 16 books published. <www.mariagillan.com>

David Giver lives in Savannah with his wife and daughter. David's collection of poems, *A Slow Education,* was just released by Shabda Press. David received his BA from the University of Vermont, and his MFA from Goddard College.

Kat Good-Schiff is the author of a poetry chapbook, *East of North,* and has published work in *Meat for Tea, PANK, Twelve Stories,* and other journals. She loves eating local veggies, reading, and riding her bike. Kat lives in Easthampton, MA and makes a living as a technical health writer.

Benjamin S. Grossberg's books are *Sweet Core Orchard* (University of Tampa, 2009), winner of the 2008 Tampa Review Prize and a Lambda Literary Award, and *Underwater Lengths in a Single Breath* (Ashland Poetry Press, 2007). His third book, *Space*

Traveler, will be published by the University of Tampa Press this year.

Meghan Guidry is a writer, and studies religion and medicine at Harvard Divinity School. Her novella *Kinesiophobia* is forthcoming from Empty City Press in 2014, as is the premiere of her first opera *The Little Blue One*. Her first novel, *Light and Skin*, was published by Empty City Press as part of the Axiom: Radnor project.

Doug Holder is the founder of the Ibbetson Street Press. He teaches writing at Endicott College and Bunker Hill Community College. For the last 30 years he has worked at McLean Hospital where among other things he conducts poetry groups for psychiatric patients.

Aaron M.P. Jackson has twice been a recipient of grants from the Puffin Foundation and he is the former Poet Laureate of Jersey City, NJ. Jackson was born in New York City, his writing often reflects his dual heritage, with a focus on themes of love and urban existence as well as all things dog. For more visit <www.middlepoet.com>

Jennifer Jean's poetry books include: *The Archivist* and *In the War*. She's released *Fishwife Tales*, a collaborative CD; her writing's appeared in *Caketrain, Tidal Basin, Poets/Artists, The Mom Egg, Denver Quarterly,* and more; she blogs for *Amirah*, an advocacy group for sex-trafficking survivors, and teaches writing at Salem State University.

Despite being the 2011-2013 Louisiana Poet Laureate, **Julie Kane** is a native of Boston. Her most recent poetry collections are *Jazz Funeral* (2009), which won the Donald Justice Poetry Prize, and *Rhythm & Booze* (2003), a National Poetry Series winner. She teaches at Northwestern State University in Natchitoches, Louisiana.

Joy Ladin, Gottesman Professor of English at Yeshiva University, has published six books of poetry, including 2012's *The Definition of Joy*, Forward Fives award winner *Coming to Life*, and Lambda

Literary Award finalist *Transmigration*. Her memoir, *Through the Door of Life: A Jewish Journey Between Genders*, was a 2012 National Jewish Book Award finalist.

Lance Larsen has published four poetry collections, most recently *Genius Loci* (Tampa 2013). He has received a number of awards, including a Pushcart Prize and a fellowship from the National Endowment for the Arts. In 2012 he was named to a five-year term as Utah's Poet Laureate. A professor at BYU, he recently directed a study abroad program in Madrid.

Joan Logghe was Santa Fe's third Poet Laureate, 2010-2012. She teaches widely from adults at Ghost Ranch Conference Center and in college, to kids in Zagreb and Minneapolis. Logghe won a National Endowment in Poetry, a Mabel Dodge Luhan Internship, and many grants from The Witter Bynner Foundation for Poetry.

Fred Marchant's *Tipping Point* won the 1993 Washington Prize and was re-issued recently in a 20th Anniversary Second Edition. He is also the author of *Full Moon Boat* and *The Looking House*, both from Graywolf Press. He is founding director of the Creative Writing Program and Poetry Center at Suffolk University.

David Mason's many books include *Ludlow, News from the Village* and *The Scarlet Libretto*. An essayist and librettist as well as a poet, he teaches at Colorado College and serves as Poet Laureate of Colorado. He is married to poet Cally Conan-Davies (a. k. a. Chrissy Mason).

Three-time Pushcart Prize winner **Jill McDonough** is the recipient of NEA, Cullman Center, and Stegner fellowships. Her books include *Habeas Corpus* (Salt, 2008), and *Where You Live* (Salt, 2012). She directs the MFA program at UMass-Boston and 24PearlStreet, the Fine Arts Work Center online.

Donnelle McGee is the author of *Shine* (Sibling Rivalry Press, 2012). His work has appeared in *Controlled Burn, Haight Ashbury Literary Journal, Permafrost, The Spoon River*

Poetry Review, and *Willard & Maple*, among others. His work has also been nominated for a Pushcart Prize.

Wesley McNair has won grants from the Rockefeller, Fulbright and Guggenheim foundations and two NEA grants in creative writing. He has twice been invited to read his poetry by the Library of Congress and was recently selected for a USA Fellowship as one of America's "finest living artists." He is the Poet Laureate of Maine.

Caryn Mirriam-Goldberg is the 2009-2013 Poet Laureate of Kansas, and the author of 16 books, including a novel, *The Divorce Girl* and *Needle in the Bone: How a Holocaust Survivor and Polish Resistance Fighter Beat the Odds and Found Each Other*. Founder of Transformative Language Arts – a master's program in social and personal transformation through the written, spoken and sung word – at Goddard College where she teaches, Mirriam-Goldberg also leads writing workshops widely.
<www.CarynMirriamGoldberg.com>

Judson Mitcham's work has been published in *Poetry, Georgia Review, Hudson Review,* and elsewhere. His most recent book is *A Little Salvation: Poems Old and New*. He is the Poet Laureate of Georgia.

Alfred Nicol's book of poetry, *Elegy for Everyone*, published in 2009, was chosen for the first Anita Dorn Memorial Prize. He received the 2004 Richard Wilbur Award for an earlier volume, *Winter Light*. His poems have appeared in *Poetry, Dark Horse, The Hopkins Review*, and other literary journals.

Oregon's sixth Poet Laureate, **Paulann Petersen** has six full-length books of poetry, most recently *Understory* from Lost Horse Press. She was a Stegner Fellow at Stanford University, and received the 2006 Holbrook Award from Oregon Literary Arts. She serves on the board of Friends of William Stafford, organizing the January Stafford Birthday Events.

Emily Pineau studies creative writing at Endicott College. Recent publications include the *Somerville News, The Endicott*

Review, Ibbetson Street, and *Muddy River Poetry Review*. Her poem "I would for you" was nominated for a Pushcart Prize in 2012. The Ibbetson Street Press published her poetry collection *No Need to Speak*.

Robert Pinsky's new book is *Singing School: Learning to Write (and Read) Poetry by Studying with the Masters*. His other recent publications include *Selected Poems* and *PoemJazz*, a CD with Grammy-winning pianist Laurence Hobgood. As three-term Poet Laureate of the United States he founded the Favorite Poem Project, with the videos at <www.favoritepoem.org>

Miriam Sagan founded and runs the creative writing program at Santa Fe Community College. Her blog is Miriam's Well <miriamswell.wordpress.com>. She is the author of twenty-five books, including *Seven Places In America: A Poetic Sojourn* (Sherman Asher, 2012).

Jan Seale, the 2012 Texas Poet Laureate, is the author of nine poetry volumes and several books of short fiction and essays. Her writing has appeared in numerous journals and anthologies, as well as on National Public Radio. Books of poetry include *Nape* and *The Wonder Is;* short fiction includes *Appearances*.

Dan Sklar teaches creative writing at Endicott College. Recent publications include the *Harvard Review, New York Quarterly,* and *Ibbetson Street Press*. His one act play "Lycanthropy" was produced at the Boston Theater Marathon in 2012 and was reviewed in the *The Boston Globe*.

Kevin Stein has published eleven books of poetry, criticism, and anthology, including his new collection *Wrestling Li Po for the Remote* (Fifth Star Press, 2013). Current Poet Laureate of Illinois, he is Caterpillar Professor of English at Bradley University.

David Trinidad's most recent books are *Dear Prudence: New and Selected Poems* (2011) and *Peyton Place: A Haiku Soap Opera* (2013), both published by Turtle Point Press. He lives in Chicago, where he teaches in the Creative Writing Department at Columbia College.

William Carlos Williams was awarded the first National Book Award for Poetry for *Paterson: Book III* and *Selected Poems*. He posthumously received the Pulitzer Prize for *Pictures from Brueghel and Other Poems*. His other books include *Imaginations*, *Spring and All* and *The Tempers*. He was also a skilled physician.

In 1860, while strolling through Boston Commons, Ralph Waldo Emerson tried to convince **Walt Whitman** to tone down *Leaves of Grass*. Whitman refused. It was banned in Boston and the District Attorney threatened the publisher. Over 150 years later, it remains one of the most popular poetry books in the world.

Margaret Young grew up in Oberlin, Ohio and studied at Yale and U. C. Davis. She has two collections of poetry, *Willow from the Willow* (Cleveland State Poetry Center) and *Almond Town* (Bright Hill Press). She teaches food ecology and creative writing at Endicott College, and lives in Beverly.

www.ingramcontent.com/pod-product-compliance
Lightning Source LLC
LaVergne TN
LVHW041635070426
835507LV00008B/646